SHE

IS

A

LIONESS

By

Kristine Andaya Ventura

COPYRIGHT @ 2021 SHE IS A LIONESS

By Kristine Andaya Ventura

Designed by Tess Ritumalta
Edited by Marie Ezekiel

ISBN:
Softbound/Paperback-978-621-470-033-2
Hardbound-978-621-470-034-9
Mobile/Kindle-978-621-470-035-6

Published by
Poetry Planet Book Publishing House
688 Rosario Pozorrubio Pangasinan 2435 Philippines
Email: maritesritumalta@gmail.com
Contact: 09554960044

Photos used courtesy of Canva.com and Pinterest containing their own copyrights.

DEDICATION

For all the mothers who buried half of their life in the
deep hole of sacrifice for the sake of their children, and
for all the migrant workers who are enduring the pain
and facing challenges overseas.

3

ACKNOWLEDGEMENT

Thank you Ate Rolinda Espanola, author of *No Cinderella, sis* Rea Maac, author of *More than Just a Shadow*, and ate Ailene Mae Ramos, author of *Beyond the Sunset*. Your motivations gave me a bunch of good thoughts on the world of poetry. Thank you again and again, *Cinderella's Angels*.

Note: "Hidden Love" was included in the collection of a poem by The Poet Magazine entitled Friends and Friendship

FOREWORD

"SHE IS A LIONESS" represents how one must be strong and wise just like a lioness hunting for food to feed her cubs. Overseas Filipino workers are lionesses in search for gold in the jungle of foreign countries to provide their families a better life…

For OFW writers, writing became their solace to fight homesickness as they cope with problems in a land unfamiliar to them … They let go of their extreme emotions through poetry that somehow helped them win such a fight for themselves.

Kristine's book reveals her battle over her depression as she journey to a foreign country while thinking of her beloved children in the Philippines. The heartaches she encountered from a failed relationship with the person she loved were mostly the topics of her poems. The discrimination and inhumane acts of subordinates every OFW experiences were all revealed in this book as well as the pain and intense loneliness they have to bear to provide their families a much comfortable life… All these sentiments are found in her poetry that will captivate and melt the readers' hearts.

The author is such a great poet that her poems are deep and haunting, "every good writer can write a poem, but only gifted poets can write heart-touching poems", Kristine is one of the few gifted poets. Who would have thought that she is among the thousand budding poets who are new in the world of writing and as she writes her feelings, she became a very effective writer and the reason this book is created.

So open the book and explore inside Kristine Andaya Ventura's thoughts while working in the land of the Malay…

The Publisher

TABLE OF CONTENTS

DEFEATED FEAR

She retains her comely,
Assuming that one day
He'll come back.
With bated breath,
She remains calm.
She waited,
Till she became
A living skeleton.
From dawn to dusk
She's at peace,
Yet none pass by.
Not even a shadow
Of that selfish man.

Heartbeats like a drum.
Sweats are frozen yet
melted by the warm body.
She kneels,
Begging for mercy.
Pleasing to be love
Even in a while.
She even offered
The whole world,
Indeed,
She became a sinner,
Yet still, he's a stone.

Her tears flow
Continuously
Knees shaking,
Trembling
While patiently waiting
For a wonderful scene
She kept on smiling
Though her pain
Was in vain
She kept on holding
Until
She learned to defeat
Her biggest fear
The fear to lose the man
Whose heart was
Made of steel.

LIKE DRY LEAVES

I am the woman who praised you like a king,
The woman wiping her tears behind the door every
night.
I am the woman that you misused,
And once lost her contentment.
I am the woman that isolated herself in gloom.
Can you remember me?

Let me remind you
How you spitted my love.
Like a spoiled dish,
You hurled me like rubbish.
Like dry leaves,
You took my heart,
You stepped on it until it crashed.
My pain was in vain.
Can you remember now?

Can you recall how you possessed me?
On how you abused my fragility
You left me
Like an empty can
My world turns gray
When I knew you betrayed me.

Yet, I forgive you
For I believe
you deserve a second chance
So again I dance

You make me spin like a spinning wheel,
you make me feel that your love was real.
And I've been devoted to you.
But I made the wrong decision.
You cheated me not once not twice,
But more than ten times.

I pleased you,
I even kneel,
I said please don't treat me like a clown,
Yet, you never listen.
You remain heartless.
And again, I forgive you.
Though I never wanted to be called a "fool".
People laugh at me,
Yes, they did and I heard
and I cried a million times.
But I ignore.
For I thought you're a knight in shining armor.

I know you remember me.
And I am assuring you,
You can no longer find someone like me.

TO LEAVE IN PEACE

If only I have a chance to choose,

I will paint my world with a rainbow

Wherein no black, no sorrow.

I want a quiet place

As calm as space

I want to stay

In a world

Without

YOU

BRIGHTER FUTURE

My past is full of failure,
I went through a lot of trouble,
Now I want to have a better future.

I am working harder and double,
Until my sweat fell on the ground,
But why my sacrifices were gone like a bubble.

Do I need to ask from the people around,
Or should I work more than a slave?
Music of success still no sound.

Maybe my future hides in a cave,
Nor floating freely in the sky,
Or maybe It's time for me to save.

I promised myself I'll try,
To brighten my future like the sky.

DEADLY ISOLATION

She sailed a hundred miles to hunt for her destiny,
But end up in a life that lacks harmony.

She explored with gladness and complete heart,
But now living with dreams that are torn apart.

Her love and faith totally decayed,
When she realized, she was betrayed.

She tried to stand with her own feet on the ground,
But the sound of success never heard around.

Battling in a world of wonders and complications,
Separates her body and mind into a different dimension.

She tried to comfort her inner soul,
But hopeless, she's stuck into a hole.

For years, she's drowning with her own tears,
Burdens kept whispering into her ears.

One night, she buried herself into deep isolation,
Wherein she got defeated by her emotion.

I'LL BE FINE

Somewhere down the unfamiliar place,
I accidentally found an empty space.
In a hurry, I went to sit,
I need to calm down my heartbeat.

As I started counting my tears,
Lost memories started to appears;
A sweet smile yet hide a lie,
And the man who makes me cry.

Tears fell like heavy rain,
I don't know how to reduce the pain.
To forget is not easy to do,
Life must give me a clue.

I closed my eyes and took a breath,
I thought, nothing to regret.
I just cuddle myself and whisper,
"I promise I'll build myself stronger.

UNDYING HOPE

An unknown virus attacked countries,

Police surround stopping parties.

People asking dying increased,

Graveyard fully buried deceased.

Stomach starving eating nothing,

Children crying begging praying.

Vaccine coming human taking,

Body testing hoping something.

Doctors nurses staying outside,

Telling kindly human inside.

Hoping someday normal again,

Living peaceful kindness retain.

PLEASE, LET ME

Let me hold your hands gently,
Let me guide you towards your destiny.
Let me be by your side, don't be alone,
Don't leave me and live on your own.

Let me be the light that brightens your mind,
Together we walk, I won't leave you behind.
Let me introduce you to the real world,
I'll teach you how to fight without using a sword.

Let me show you how much I care,
I want you to feel the true love of a mother.
Let me teach you what is right and wrong,
Let me mold you how to be strong.

Let me prepare for you a better future,
Let me teach you how to face failure.
One of these days I'll be gone,
Please give me a chance, I want all this to be done.

VOICE OF A MIGRANT

We work more than you pay,
We must do whatever you'll say.
Didn't you ever think that we're human?
We have flesh like you, we are human.

You can scold us if we have a mistake,
But you can't ask why our smile is fake.
You can scream as loud as you can,
But you don't have the right to hurt us
    with your hand.

You don't give us delicious foods, it's ok,
You let us wear old clothes, it still ok.
Yet give us some privacy,
And don't torture us mentally.

For you our dignity is priceless,
But for us, it is a diamond to be cherished.
Shield us and we will serve you,
Treat us good and we will obey you.

We are migrant workers
We work harder
We dream bigger
We became stranger
We are great migrant workers.

SHE IS ME

She, maybe speechless sometimes,
But deep in the darkness of her room,
She's scolding herself silently.

She, maybe smiling so sweet to you,
But in her heart, she hides the bitter part.
She probably feels pitty now for herself.

She, who wants you to have a wonderful life,
Working patiently with all her power.
She, maybe tired now but still you can't see.

She may be screaming most of the time,
Teaching you what is right and wrong.
She can be your best friend forever.

She, who sacrifices herself for your happiness,
Can you cuddle her when you see her
crying?
She, who can give you love and care.
She's your mother,
She is me.

LONGING HEART

As I look at the stars in the sky,
I wished to have the power to fly.
As I stared at the bright moon,
I wished to be back home soon.

My heart stops beating,
My tears kept on falling.
I can't think nicely,
I really missed my family.

My closed eyes are searching,
I can hear though I am sleeping.
Their gigglings echoed in my brain,
Their smile has the power to ease my pain.

As the wind wipe my tears,
I also take away my fears.
I may be far from them now,
I know, one day I will go back somehow.

HOMELESS BUT NOT HOPELESS

along the river banks, she chooses
cardboard and trash, she used
with weakened arms but strong faith
little paradise, she builds

her heart is full of determination
living alone with the stones
only sun rays brighten her dark room
not knowing until when she will live alone

walking barefoot on the street
begging for someone who can feed
this homeless girl, longing for love
hoping on her way she could find

with our naked eyes, we can see
an innocent face who lost her family
inside of her is full of positivity
that one day she can find the home
where she is supposed to live.

Once in a dark night
thunder and lightning occur,
her little paradise
washed out by the storm.
teardrops fall on the ground
but her faith was never gone,
"I may lose my home
but not my hope"

she whispered
as she breathes so deep.

behind her sorrow, she smiles
like the sun peeping through the dark clouds,
her eyes shine like a rainbow
hoping for a brighter tomorrow.

once again she picks some trash,
and decided to rebuild her paradise.
with a weakened body
she makes it stronger as she could,
For if one day
she finds her family,
they have a place
to sleep peacefully.

This little girl was once
homeless but not hopeless.

THE TRUTH BEHIND

I heard a loud voice last night,
I thought there is a huge fight.

When I came out of the darkroom,
I saw the mad face of the groom.

I felt a mixture of nervous and worried,
Though I am not the one who will get married.

Walking towards me was the bride,
Shivering. Should I move aside?

Her face was covered with confusion,
She's panicking, full of emotion.

She cried so bad asking for my forgiveness,
Her confession covered my world with darkness.

She said "He is the man you supposed to marry,
But on that special day, you lost your memory.

I felt so sorry for what I heard,
Yet I remain calm like a humming bird.

He can no longer be mine, I need to set him free,
This girl in front of me is carrying a baby.

It hurts but I open my heart and mind,
I need to accept all the truth behind.

SLAVE NOT MAID

You treated her as a slave, not a maid,
Never at once, you show humanity.
Is it because she's well paid?

In a dark room where she stayed,
She tried to protect her comely.
You treated her as a slave, not a maid.

"You're just nothing" you always said.
Why can't you show some generosity,
Is it because she's well paid?

She is always uncomfortable and afraid.
Where is equality?
You treated her as a slave, not a maid.

She works more than a housemaid,
Yet you underestimate her ability.
Is it because she's well paid.

You always think you've been betrayed.
Not knowing what's her real identity,
You treated her as a slave, not a maid.
Is it because she's well paid?

HEAVEN BY YOUR SIDES

The smile in your eyes
 are stars
that blinks in the night.
The way you say,
"I Love You, mama"
melts my heart.
You are the reason why
my bones are firm and strong.
Having you by my side
is heaven.

I am a tree
and you're the sunlight
giving me the energy to live.
I am dry land
and you're the rain,
Watering my soul
and made me live again.
You are the wind
beneath my wings.

My heart broke
when I left you.
My soul is crying,
I really missed you.
And if the day comes
that I can hug you again,
For sure I will float in the sky.
To be by your side is heaven.

FOOLISH HEART

As we walk through the isle
I saw your evil eye.
I was puzzled,
I want to run away.
I ask myself,
Is it because of contentment,
Or hidden doubt
Or maybe disappointment.

In front of the altar, we vow,
We'll survive no matter what.
Together we made promises,
Each second and minute,
We will cherish it.
Together,
We exchanged our ring,
Symbolized that we are taken.

Yes, I do love you,
With all my heart
I accepted you.
With all my heart
I gave my life,
Even your tongue
Was sharp as a knife.

I will love you till the end,
I will love you till my backbone bend.
I will love you,
Thou your words fooled my heart.
For we both promised,
"Till death do us part".

ACCUSATIONS AND LIES

I knew her as a loving daughter,
Her hands are wide open to give extra care.
I knew her as a good mother,
Willing to die for her sons and daughter.
I knew her many years ago,
And I can't believe what my naked eyes saw.

I saw when you screamed to her like hell,
On how you pointed your middle finger.
I saw when she begged you to calm down,
But you're indeed a stone-hearted man.
I saw when she cried almost every night,
When the kids are sleeping so tight.

And I heard;

I heard on how you humiliated her,
You told me that she's a useless mother.
I heard when you say " You're nothing",
But I know, she did everything.
I heard when you throw your bad words,
Yet she remained calm even her heart feels ripped by the
sword.

I heard and I saw a lot of happenings
And I know,
You accused her to cover up your lies.

HIDDEN LOVE

Wearing a mask of sorrow,
I walk with my shadow.
With a weakened body,
I continued my journey.
Not knowing where to go,
I kept on going through.

You found me helpless,
Amid darkness.
You held my hand slowly,
You lift me up gently.
Out of the blue, I cried,
Those pains can no longer hide.

You lend your ears,
You wipe away my tears.
You said"trust me, my dear"
Yet, I refused because of fear.

You took me to an open door,
And guided me as we explore.
You let me in into an open hall,
Where in my face painted on the wall.

Now I know why you always care,
Now I know why you're always there.
You're my soulmate, sent from above.
Thank you for the hidden love.

STILL, I AM HERE

Here in a foreign land,
I became a stranger.
Nobody knows the pain that I feel,
On how I am surviving here.
Nobody knows when my wounds will get heal,
Either the scars that are hidden with seal.
Nobody knows, no one can understand,
Even I reveal.
But still, I am here.

I left my comfort zone,
To fulfill my dreams and goals.
I left my children to earn dollars,
but before I have it, I must listen to their unending roars.
Even I feel so tired and my body is shakin',
I can't refuse, It is a must to clean.
But still, I am here.

I am here to sacrifice,
Not enjoying in a paradise.
I am here serving other people,
While my family is longing for me.
I am here as their maid,
Sometimes treated like a slave.
Still, I am here,
I am here, but not forever.

DEPRESSION, A SILENT KILLER

A lady drowned with fears.
A pillow that flooded with tears,

Loud voices aroused.
She got mad,
It is bugging her ears.
In the midst of battle,
Enemies are everywhere.
Roar by her masters,
The longing of her parents,
And mostly,
cries of her children.

The wind carried her,
Somewhere,
but no one is aware.
She tried to comfort herself,
But she can't control it at all.
Up the highest floor,
she climbed,
Out of her mind,
she jumped.
Her body lay on the ground,
Breathless,
With a broken head.
Her warm blood showered her.

No more pain,
No more stress.
Now she's resting in peace.
Everything is ended,
But family will suffer.
Depression defeated her.
Depression, a silent killer.

SILENT CRY

His arms are steel
palms were rough as sand;
Until he can't even stand
He's working without a meal.

He's melting under the flammable sun
and tears flow like heavy rain;
Yet he stays calm and endures the pain
but paid less by the heartless man.

He sends his salary immediately
leaving his pocket empty
just to pull them out from poverty
Yet still betrayed by beloved family.

Deep inside his heart hides a big lie
saying he's fine but he's not!
behind the door, he suffered a lot,
but no one heard his silent cry.

WHY I REMAINED SILENT

I remained silent for how many years,
Every night, my room submerged with
tears;
I chose to be silent not because of fears
I zipped up my mouth yet I opened my heart and ears.

In any circumstances, I left no comment,
I let him think that I am an innocent;
On the other hand, I hate nonsense arguments,
So I'd rather shut up my mouth and
persist the silence.

Million of concepts filled my mind,
A vacant area can no longer find;
My heart was deluged with sorrow
Yet I still need to survive for tomorrow.

I remained silent and try not to wound my feeling,
I always think that every difficulty has an ending;
I'd rather focus on my aim, I know I will be fine,
Instead of roaring to a person that can no longer be mine.

How I Wish

How I wish to reside peacefully,
In a place guarded by love and harmony;
How I wish I am utterly free,
Away from a chaotic community.

I am pondering how flying birds feels like,
Are they contented or scared to be struck?
How about a peaceful hike,
Or a voyage using a motorbike.

Dozens of leaves descend from the tree,
While flowers are blooming magically;
How I wish I am a butterfly,
Freely flying under the wondrous sky.

I wonder how fish survived underwater,
Are they getting tired or they don't bother;
How I wish I could be like a ferry,
Freely sailing on the deep blue sea.

How I wish to sleep on a silent night,
While cuddling my daughters so tight;
Oh how I wish this world was war free,
All unite with humanity and dignity.
Kristine removed a message

SHE'S GONE WITH THE MUSIC

I was amazed by the way she dressed.
Beads are glittering,
eyes are glowing.
She looked so elegant, like brilliant.
Her lips are red "Can I kiss" suddenly I
whispered.
Her cheeks
turned to a cherry color.

I held her hand
and pulled her body near me.
I can smell the perfume,
it's everywhere inside the room.
Her face near to my face,
"Give me space" she whispered.
She took my breath away.

I started to move,
I step forward.
You step backward,
I step backward.
You step forward,
together we danced.
"Don't look behind "I said.
Yet she's stone-hearted.

She stopped the music,
And left me in the midst of the hall.
My happiness was replaced with tears.
She held his hand and walk away.
Then they go, together again.
Can I have one more chance"
I cried.

HALL OF SORROW

When you smashed your promises,
My heart crushed into pieces.
You left me drowning with fear,
And leave everything unclear.

I will love you till the end of the day,
What should I do to make you stay?
My world collapsed when you walk away,
It's killing me softly day by day.

You harm my whole body,
Leaving with a pinch of dignity.
How dare you, why you hurt me so badly.
I'd rather live alone like a scarecrow,
Than to be locked in the hall of sorrow.

TILL I MOURN

The whole day
  I was on fire
    Behind the trees
      Seeking on you

The whole day
  I shine brightly
    I wipe your tears
      I make you sweat

The whole day
  I stunt in the gloom
    I kept waiting
      Till I mourn.

JUST LET GO

If your mind filled with worries,
Go outside, feel the cold breeze.

If you're bothered with annoying scenarios,
Scream silently, let go of your sorrows.

If your feet feel so tired of walking,
Just think that you're on the clouds, floating.

If your eyes longing for wonders,
Open your windows and wave to the angels.

If your bare hands are empty and free,
Take a note of anything you can see.

If you feel that your heart isn't complete,
Take some of your time, give yourself a treat.

Let go of all your emotions in the air,
Don't make your life a nightmare.

Look, the world created with love,
Live freely like how birds are exploring above.

Let go of anything that bothered you,
Let go, just let it go.

A WALK IN HEAVEN

I went to heaven,
Wherein, I found peace.
Tiny grasses were rejoicing,
Birds are singing so gently,
Trees are dancing gracefully.
My heart starts jumping,
My eyes are rolling,
I kept on wondering.
Suddenly
cold breeze kissed me.
My knees shake,
Butterflies came and comfort me,
then Mr. Sun smiled widely.
I was an angel exploring above,
I really felt great love.
Oh! How nice to live in heaven.
I closed my eyes.
When I was about to sit on the clouds,
I fell.
I started to feel pain.
Only I realized,
I am climbing on a tree,
While my eyes closed tightly.

BE LIKE LION

Live like a lion,
   Always wear faith.
      Obey your heart,
         Fight for your life.

Be mindful,
   Protect yourself.
      Roar if needed,
         Walk with respect.

Be humble,
   Listen carefully.
      Act like a human,
         Think wisely.

ELUSIVE DREAM

In the midst of the deep blue
   sea,
A huge ship awaits me.
Curiosity and frightened,
that's what I
  feel. Suddenly
Shadow came to me.
Come on lady,
  let's have a walk.
Shivering.
I'm stuck,
   can't even talk.

Holding her hands,
She held me inside.
I'm amazed,
It's paradise.
Wonderful creatures
   surround, Hearts
beat so loud.

I swim with whales,
I run barefoot with
   lioness,
Bird sings a lullaby,
As I fly up to the
  sky. Next
is jumping on the tallest
  fall,

But a loud voice awakes me.
I scared.
I scream,
Oh! It's
   Only an elusive dream.

BLESSING'S COMING

Hopeful mother praying daily,

Alone working earning money.

Wearing patience fighting firmly,

Bringing kindness towards the journey.

Heartless human, looking, laughing,

Sometimes spitting mercy nothing.

Loving mother hoping wishing,

After sorrow blessing's coming.

MASK, NO MORE

I was once addressed as " stupid".
I smile even they spit on me;
I let them stamped on my dignity.
I smile even their expressions hurt me;
Words that ripped my heart,
Words that thorn my character apart.
I let them! Yes, I let them.

Wearing a fake mask,
I walk alone.
I face the world,
I fight on my own.
I let them laugh at me,
I let them humiliate me.

But now,
I am better.
I take out that mask,
I uncover my face.
I learned to face the truth,
I walk with strength and faith.

I am better now!
No need to pretend.
I can face the world,
Without wearing a mask.

PARADISE OF SACRIFICE

Foreign land! Foreign land.
A place where dreams do come true!
Millions and millions of people are
pursuing to go,
Not knowing, what life awaits.

Poverty! Poverty, poverty.
The main reason why we left our family.
A better future is our aim
Nobody knows our pain.
Others thought,
We're having a marvelous life,
Yes! A magnificent life.

No one knows know that;

Tears! Tears and tears.
Crystal water that kept falling on our cheeks,
Letting it flow is the easiest way to ease our longingness,
Mostly to our kids.

A foreign land is a paradise,
But you can't go if you can't sacrifice.

YOU HEAL ME

I waited
   till he appears.
      From dawn to dusk
         I never leave.

I waited
   till the raindrops
      wet the whole ground,
         I feel so down.

I waited
   until you pass by.
      You touched my heart
         and healed me.

BAG OF GOODIES

I've never seen her
for a couple of years,
So when I saw her,
I got fear.
I am afraid
she might cry.
I am afraid
she may ask me, why.
Why I am with her?
I tried not to make her upset,
Nor to feel that I am another.
I comfort her when she's sad,
Thou I don't know how
to make her calm when she's mad.
I loved to be with her,
So anywhere we go,
I have my bag.
A bag that she loves to hug.
A bag that full of goodies
To make her smile.
A bag that she can open
when she's angry or hungry.

HOW AM I TODAY?

I am lone with
my plans,
I don't know how to end
nor where to start.

My dreams
is only to be with them,
I left, even my heart
filled with condemnation.

In times of sadness
I choose to smile,
Even behind
were stories that can't compile.

You may see me
waking with courage,
But my mind and soul
abandoned in a cage.

Sunrise may shine
before I get up,
Definitely, I'll continue my journey,
I won't stop.

I am ok, that's
only I can say,
If ever you'll ask
"How are you today?

SUNSET, STAY WITH ME

You're so wonderful,
You have shown up
in a mysterious way.
Your figure glazed,
I am always amazed.

I always wonder why
at night you're gone,
Where are you hiding
when the day is done?
without staring at you,
I won't last the day.
Hoping that tomorrow
I will see you through.

Oh sun that setting
I wished you can hear,
My burdens and pain
I whispered in your ears,
Burn it nicely,
turn them into dust.
Oh sun that setting
can you stay next to me,
Don't let anyone steal
or step on my dignity.

RAIN

Oh, rain pour! Shower me till I drowned.

Agony, can't endure at all.

Pour! Don't let them spit at me,

Help me to end this fear.

Pour! Cuddle my soul.

Make me feel free.

I need you.

Hear me,

Rain.

NO ONE KNOWS ME

I used to drink my tears all this while,

If I got hurt, I will just cry.

I never talk back at all,

Even they hurled my heart.

Nobody knows me,

Nor what I feel.

Nobody,

Except

Me

FEARLESS SNAKE

Here in my quiet kingdom,
I lay.
The only space
where I can stay.
Here, I am safe.
Here, my heart is at peace.
You can pass by,
any time you want.
Just don't disturb me
Or else
I can be your worst enemy.
Indeed,
I can bring your life in danger.

I loved to explore
Greeneries I really adore.
I tried to stand up,
I want to see the beauties that surround,
But I can't,
Nobody wants to accompany me.
If only I have wings to fly
to soar and reach the sky.
How I wish
I can continue my journey,
But the outside world
Never welcome me.

NEW YEAR, NEW LIFE

Magnificent Monday morning.
I packed a pair of pants,
Some shirts, shoes, and slippers.
Paradise of Penang probably preparing.

Shimmering sun showing up so slowly.
Whistling wind, whispered come cuddle me.
I was patiently picking seashells on the seashore
With a heart-humming and sweet smile.
Its beauty is the best, I really adored.

A forest that full of flowers and fern.
Green grasses growing on the ground.
Tall trees are waiving while we're walking.
I thought I was only dreaming.

Despite being far from my family,
I extremely enjoyed the scenery.
Twenty-twenty one officially open its door,
Let's live and love our life to the fullest.

A good and great start this year.
New year, new life, new me.

TO BE LOVED BY YOU

When we are in High School,
I already knew.
Something you're hiding, don't you?
You tried to become a friend of mine,
But I ignore you, and I feel sorry for that.

After a long journey, 13 years to be exactly
We met again in a place called "Social Media"
I never thought I can see again,
Those smile that once I never bother.

I thought it is just for fun.
To have an affair with you, wasn't easy.
But a couple of years had already passed,
Hopefully, this will forever last.

We often have misunderstandings like kids,
But it will last only a couple of minutes,
We don't end up the day without talking to each other,
Especially if one of us is really full of anger.

Thank you for giving me a space in your life,
For motivating me that everything will be alright,
Thank you for letting me show you how much I care.
Having You in my life makes me stronger.

BRAVE SOUL WINS

demon dragging down
failure demolishing dreams
but mind enlighten by a clear vision

trials threatened yet never give up
people humiliated like hell
still, risen like sun

darkness crawled and cuddled
frustration and fade visions occur
yet still, bloom like a wild flower

accusations were hanging on walls
screaming to hang up bodies
yet like the sky, calmness retain

problems hammering head
darkness hypnotizes minds
but still, brave soul wins

HELPLESS MOTHER

I'm a mother,
A soft-hearted mother.
A mother,
That no one supposes to hurt.
I'm not a slave,
For a man,
A man with no heart.

Anybody,
I need someone.
Who can understand
my unspoken words?
I can talk,
But I can't
express it.
I don't know
How?
Anyone
can lend an ear,
Who can listen
to my heartbeat?

I'm
A mother,
I have the right
to fight for my rights.
I
Who Have feelings,
I am also,

human being.
Listen
to me.

yes
I have weaknesses, But
No one
Can make me
Shameless.
I know,
I'm strong,
As strong as a stone.That
No one can break
My bone.
I know
I can
stand by
my own.

WHEN NO ONE CARES

I saw her sitting.
Her eyes were staring at nowhere.
Suddenly she bows her head,
And put her palm on the face.

With a soft voice, I ask her why.
What happens? Are you alright?
Slowly she looked at me and gasp,
"I am fine, and I will be fine".
But I know, something is running
on her mind.

"Can you see those people",
suddenly she asks.
Why they treating me
like a wind?
Can't they feel
that I am here?
Or should I shout
for them to hear?
I want them to know
what I really feel.
I can't see that their love
for me is real.
I feel like
I am always behind.
No one's paying attention to me.
No one protects me.

My teardrops fall.
I can't touch but I can feel her.
I can see myself to her.
I lift her face.
I know her.
Yes.
I really knew.
That lady
is no other than
Me.

SHADOW OF THE PAST

It's dark cold midnight.
Yet still, my presence was awake.
I was there,
But my mind is miles away.
Standing, talking to the moon.
Searching in the meadow for nothing.
Something is bothering me.

The silence of the room,
it's bugging my ears.
My heart beats like a drum,
Hands are sweating,
My knees are shaking.
A lot of things
are running on my mind.

As I closed my wide eyes,
I saw you.
You and your dark shadow.
A cold breeze touched my soul.

The pictures of the past,
They are coming back again.

I don't want to be a prisoner,
Nor to remember those scars.
I don't want to get stuck.
I don't want to leave,
with the shadow of the past.

MY LITTLE WISH

Dearest ones,
I miss you so badly
I want to hug,
and kiss you gently.
But I can't,
I'm miles away.
All I can do is think
and pray that you are ok.

Your loving arms,
I really missed it.
Dearest ones,
I am dying for your love.
You are the best treasure
that I have.

It is difficult for me
to think that you are far,
Like a dreamer,
dreaming to touch the stars.
Counting days and months,
I always do.

If I have a wish only for tonight,
I will ask to come to your dream
so I can hug you tight,
That even in your dreams
I want you to feel,
That I love you,
and I miss you so.

GOD'S MESSAGE

Once I am alone, I ask God why,
Why are you letting people cry?
God looked at me and answered,
"Don't worry, I won't let you suffer".

I said, "Can't you see people are struggling.
Most of us can't survive, really suffering.
The Lord replied with bright eyes,
"Don't worry, everything will be alright."

"LORD," I said with a bit of anger.
How could you said You won't let us suffer?
People are starving, no food to eat,
Some are just picking rubbish on the street.

The Lord said with a soft voice,
"These disasters are people's choices.
You abuse the gift of nature,
Now you're blaming me for this failure.

I am speechless, don't know what to say,
Forgive me, I'm too hash today.
Who Am I to tell you those words,
I am your creature, and You are my Lord.

The Lord said:
"Love the nature as you love me,
All of these are my creativity,
I used my hands to make it perfect,
Don't destroy. GIVE A LITTLE RESPECT.

I swear

When I lost you,
My heartbreaks
into pieces.
My life became
so messy
and miserable, But
when you're gone,
Everything is fine
and stable.

I let you go,
I set you free,
Coz everything I do,
Wasn't good enough
for you.

To myself,
I made a promise. That
I will forget you,
No matter how long it takes.

I swear
upon the blue sky,
I don't want
to see you again,
Until the day that
my life is done.

THE ONE I LOST

I loved her the most,
But I made a mistake,
A nightmare indeed.

I was exploring, really enjoying it.
Not knowing I am already annoying.
I hang up with my friends,
Going here and there.
I kept on doing those,
Not knowing she's watching.
She never asks for precious things,
Nor to travel anywhere.
She just asks some couple of times,
Which is free but I can't give.

I thought she won't give up,
But I was wrong.
Without saying a word,
She stepped out of the door.
I don't know I hurt her,
I made her cry.
I never realized,
I broke her heart into pieces.

I lost the girl
that I want to live with.
I lost the girl
who completed my life.
I lost the girl
that once I called, wife.
Now I am living alone.

DAUGHTER'S LOVE

Her colorful world turns gray,
When they said, "Your father passed away."

Sitting at the edge of the bed, she cried,
The pain in her heart can no longer hide.

Without thinking twice, she asks God why
"Why all your promises turn to lie?

Can't do anything but to stay by her side,
I've just said "I know He will be your guide.

With a teary eye, she said "I am letting him go,
I know I am strong and I can keep on going through.

Looking at her father's remains, she prayed.
She promised that in her heart he will stay.

So, with her blessings she said goodbye,
"I'll meet you again, once I will die."

YOUR MEMORIES WILL REMAIN

As I closed my eyes,
I remember your face
laying you on a white bed.
You're surrounded by beautiful
colorful flowers
and scented candles.

As I think of you
my dear grandma,
teardrops fall like heavy rain.
I can't express the pain
that I felt inside
why you need
to left us behind.

I also remember
when I was in Grade Four,
We always go to the river
Happily washing clothes together.
We used to bake cassava cake
and never scold me
whenever I make a mistake.

How I wish
you're still alive,
I want you to witness
how can I survive?
But I know
wherever I go

You are always there
to guide me through.

Oh grandma
I missed you.
I want to hug you once again.
I want you to know
that I love you,
and you will always be
in my heart.
Till we meet again grandma.

Kneel in front of me,

Right now if you want my mercy.

Is it unfair if I'll be rude?

Staying calm can no longer do.

Time has come to set myself free,

Indeed you don't deserve my beauty.

Not at all, I'll beg for you to come back.

Enough is enough.

#acrostic

ABECEDARIAN OF THE PHILIPPINES

Absolutely amazing!

Beaches are wide and blue,

Coral reefs are visible too.

Davao is where the President resides,

Energetic and brave that's how he is.

Forests are full of wild animals,

Green grasses and tall trees surround.

Halo-halo is the best dessert I've eaten,

Ingredients are mainly sweetened.

Jones Isabela is the place where I was

  born and

Kristine is my respective name.

Landscapes are made with love, wherein

Magnificent views can be done.

Nipa house is the best place to rest

Or in a treehouse where birds have nest.

Philippines, my beloved country. I am

Quietly watching how you grow.

Rain or shine, farmers are working,

Sincerity is always in their heart.

Thousands of tourists visit you daily,

The universe is so proud of your beauty.

Venice Grand Canal in Taguig was so

  attractive,

Waving a million people to step on it.

Xenophobia can no longer feel, surely

Your heart will be filled with joy, so

Zip up your luggage and let's go home...

There is more fun in the Philippines...

FOREIGN LAND

Without knowing what awaits us,
We came to this foreign land.
We have dreams for our family,
We have to support them financially.

Each of us works harder and harder,
The more we work, the more we get tired.
Some of us don't have proper rest,
Longing to go back on their own nest.

We are migrants who left our families behind.
Working from sunrise 'till sunset.
Each night we go to sleep,
Without our family next to us.

Our hands are not made of steel.
Pain, that's what we always feel.
You may see us laughing,
But deep inside our hearts, we're crying.

No one knows 'till when we'll be here.
No one knows what kind of life we have.
But we know, one day we'll be going home
We'll go back where our hearts belong.

YOU'RE ALWAYS WITH ME

As I sit on the swing,
I felt I am a queen.
Guarded by giant trees,
Surrounded by greeneries.
From far I can hear,
those birds
humming without fear.
From far I can see,
those tiny creatures
exploring nature.
There, I can feel
that your love for me is real.
I can feel your hugs
send by the wind,
I can hear you whispering
I love you.
I can feel you
wherever I go,
And you know,
inside my heart is only you.

PLEASE ACCEPT MY FORGIVENESS

When I was in my mother's womb,
I can feel his hands touching me.
I can feel his love.
When I came out,
I saw his brilliant eyes,
He was drowning in the ocean of happiness.
My mom said,
I used to sleep on his arms.
He sang me a lullaby
And I heard that.

While I am enjoying my journey,
He suddenly left me.
He never saw how I grow till I became a teenage girl.
He never saw me marching on the stage.
He never saw me falling in love for the first time.
He doesn't even know what I feel right now.
I got married without him.

But those happenings are not a reason to hate him.
I never hate him at all.
I never let him feel that I got hurt.
I never let him know that many times I needed him,
that I need his loving arms to lean on.

He's one of the reasons why I became strong.
He's one of the reasons why I love my own family.
He's one of the reasons why I keep on forgiving others.
He's one of the reasons why I am a soft-hearted woman.
And he's the reason why I am here in this world.

I want to let him know;
    Thank you for giving me life.
    Thank you for giving me eyes to see
      how   wonderful is the world,
    Thank you for letting me hear those
      wonderful songs,
    Thank you for letting me feel the cold breeze,
    Thank you father for everything.
    Please accept my forgiveness.

WHY YOU'RE HERE?

Time passed by
Though memories left behind.

Time passed by like thunder and lightning,
But the wound in my soul remained.

Time passed by like a river, It continues flowing.
Not like me, sometimes stopped breathing.

Time passed by mysteriously,
Like you, just came but never stay.

Time passed by like a shooting star,
Just like you,
In a blink of an eye, you left me a scar.

Time will pass by and never come back,
But why you? You came back, trying to take my heart.
Kristine removed a message
Kristine removed a message

SOUND OF QUIETNESS

The old lake was waving, boats await to sail,
But the waste of time, none came to stay but snail;
The black squirrel climbed and sat on the tree with style,
But cute cub roar and poor pet fell with
smile.
Oh, poor old lake you're blessed with beauty,
But none can see except the old oak tree;
And the owl that sleeping so deeply.

Before, they often come to visit your view,
But now they lost their memory of how they met you;
They even forgot the place they used to sit,
They abandoned you, now full of rubbish and shit.
Oh, poor old lake no one can feel your loneliness,
None can see your heart that filled with emptiness;
Alone, you're living with the sound of quietness.

ETERNALLY

Do you remember who you are?
Do you know once in a while you're looking at your
scar;
Do you remember who makes you cry?
Do you know the reason why?
Do you know deep in the darkness you stay alone,
Dying, while thinking with that man whose heart was
stone.
Do you know inside my heart, you own a special throne?

Inside my heart there's paradise and you're the queen,
My shoulders are free whenever you want to lean;
I care for you more than anyone and I want you to know,
My love for you is clear, so pure, as white as snow;
Forget the one who hurt and ignored your feeling,
Forgive and set yourself free, for he is also a human
being.
You're special and I'll be loving you, eternally.

BITTER MEMORIES

You smiled,
but I know it's a lie.

Every moment I'll go to rest,
Your eyes were following me.
Each moment I will eat,
You stare at my plate.

If I am on call with my family,
You're pointing and yelling at me.
Why are you doing this?
What do you think of me?

I am not a machine.
I also have a bone like you,
I have flesh and can feel tired too.
All my sacrifices are nothing
Because you think I am just nothing.

Yes I know, you're diamond,
Shining above the earth.
And me, I am only a grass,
Crawling so badly on the ground.

Time will come that I will leave,
But I won't bring those bitter memories.
Never I won't forget that one day,
Our paths crossed in the same way.

SHE DESERVES RESPECT

Her smile sparks like a brilliant,
She is a good-hearted migrant.

She is a woman who walks with dignity,
She shares love unconditionally.

Her heart was filled with kindness,
She lives away from darkness.

She walks so humble as you can see,
Filling her life with good memory.

She is a woman who never gives up,
No matter how difficult, she won't stop.

She's a woman who deserves respect,
Although her life wasn't that perfect.

DARK CLOUDS

Above me
  is wondrous sky
    who's watching me
      through the day.

The blue sky
  knows my failure
    my happiness
      and who I am.

Yet dark clouds
  tried to shade the sun
    that gave me light
      to survive.

FORBIDDEN LOVE

We never had a chance,
to be with you at night
is only in our own paradise.

We never had a chance,
to walk in public
is only a choice.

We never had a chance,
to reside freely in your heart
is only a wish that is never granted.

We never had a chance,
to cuddle each other like a kids
is only in an elusive dream.

We never had a chance,
to take care of each other
is forbidden.

If only we have a chance,
We want a peaceful life
Forever.

HOME AND PARADISE

Highlands,
Beauty spot,
Away from the city.
Crowned by tall trees,
Covered with greeneries.
Climbed by mountaineers,
Discovered by adventurers.

Homes are build everywhere,
Even on a slope, it doesn't matter.
Never think about their safety measure,
As long as they live peacefully,
For them, it's a treasure.

But what if there is a tragedy,
How they can save their family?
Most houses are just made of wood
Building a home, made of stone, they can't afford.

If only I can rebuild their house,
I will do it without a second thought.
I will make it very strong,
That cannot move even by a strong storm.

I will put it very high,
On a place that is closed to the sky.
I want them to see the beauty of nature from above,
Space showed respect and love.

I'll paint it like a rainbow,
So they can smile even there is sorrow.
I'll design it like a castle, a small size,
And they will call it their own paradise.

FOR THE LAST CHANCE

Take me by your side.
Take my breath.
Pull me closer to your body.
Keep your eyes locked on mine,
And let the music be our guide.

Take my hand.
Hold it tight,
Never let it go.
Let's dance to the music of life.
I promised that I won't forget,
This moment that we shared.
I want to dance with you
Until my last breath

Take my heart.
Let those living things,
Witness our love.
Let them dance with us.
Let the trees sway its branches,
Let those falling leaves showered us with their blessings.

Take my hand,
Let's dance peacefully.
The birds are flying,
singing so gently.
Let their voice
take away our worries.

Take my hand, my dear,
Let's dance gracefully.
Let the blue skies
And the green grasses decorate our paradise.
Let us feel the fresh air,
The cold breeze that wraps in our body.

For the last chance, let's dance.

WILDFLOWERS

Wonderful creatures watching by
   the blue skies,

Isolated, living in a hidden paradise.

Leaves are growing slowly, so green,

Dancing gracefully with the wind.

Flowers are blooming in different
   colors,
Lovely hummingbirds offering their
   songs,

Oh, your beauty was really unseen.

Wildflowers you're free to grow,

Except in open space where humans
   see you through.

Rain may shower you unexpectedly,

Soon, the sun will rise to dry you nicely

#acrostic

DEAREST MAN

We are women, more precious than gold,
We can appear like a diamond.

We are women, treat us like crystal glass.
Handle us with extra love and care, it is a must.

We are women, don't break nor tear our hearts,
And we don't deserve to keep in the dark.

We are women whose real sacrifices were unseen,
Only you believe the one you see on the screen.

We are women, never torture us,
We are women whom you must trust.

We, women, are soft-hearted humans.
We are not born to serve only the man.

We are women, and empowering women,
We are not just any woman.

JUST LIKE A DUST

There's a part of my life that I am lost.
There's a part that I made my ghost.
There's a part that I want to die,
And that part when you left me behind.

I cried and cried until the day is done,
I thought after I cried the longingness will go.
I cried and I cried until I got tired,
But no matter how I cried,
I can't express the feeling that I hide.

Day by day I am begging the sun to bring you back
home,
That one day I wake up with you by my side.
Day by day I talk to the wall, counting how many days
more.
Hoping that one day you'll come back.

Night after night, I am staring at the moon.
Wishing that you'll be coming soon.
Night after night,
I am pleasing myself to be patient,
Hoping that one night will be tonight.

I will keep on loving you.
I will love you till the end.
I will love you till the moon and sun meet.
I will love you, even you treated me just like dust.

GOD ANSWERED HER PRAYER

I saw her walking alone
while staring at the phone.
Her face is so sad
I can feel how heavy the problem she had.
Suddenly she stopped
and looked at the sky above.
She opened her arms widely
and took a breathe so deeply.
And I...
I was behind her, watching secretly.

She put her hands down
and continued walking towards the town.
I was really curious,
I know she's not fine.
So I walked fast
even my feet are struggling because of thick mud.
I was about to ask if she is ok.
But then a fast car went and hit her.
In a blink of an eye,
She flew away and landed
on green grass that full of bushes.
I run so fast as I can.

I witnessed a very shocking scene.
I screamed for help but no one can lend an ear.
She's a victim of a hit and runs.
That heartless man just vanished away.
"Go to hell" I shouted with anger

I tried to carry her and said:
"Hold on my friend, this is not the end.
Slowly she holds my face and whispered:
God answered my prayer.
My teardrops fall, my hands are shaking.
I don't know what to do.
Rescuers came to save her, but it's late.
She gives up her last breathe.

On my way home someone called
and I got shocked at what she told me.
"That lady is a cancer patient miss,
she suffered a lot from that disease.
She attempts to kill herself many times
but always failed.
I never noticed that I opened my mouth and replied.
"What a very sad story.
Now I know why,
At her last minute, she said,
"God has answered her prayer.
She is resting now peacefully.
No more pain that killing her slowly.

PROVINCIANA

She's a girl who lives in a peaceful village
Surrounded by mountains and river
But so sad, she worked at her young age

A small room served as her cage
Her strength is less to work harder
She's a girl who lives in a peaceful village

Her fear end up when she saw a stage
There, she proved that she's a fighter
But so sad, she worked at her young age

She loved to stay in a small cottage
Provinciana, that is how they called her
She's a girl who lives in a peaceful village

Everyone amazed at her unique image
Her dreams make her stronger
But so sad, she worked at her young age

Yet for humiliation, she belongs to the garbage
This provinciana became a big dreamer
She's a girl who lives in a peaceful village
But so sad, she worked at her young age

APPRECIATE, WE ARE ALIVE

The world was overflowed with treasure,
Explore and enjoy the beauty of nature.
Open your eyes widely and you will see,
How lovely is God's creativity.

Life is too short so be great
Stand up, don't just lay on the bed.
Look around and feel the fresh air,
Enjoy the Gift of nature.

Encourage yourself to face all the failures,
It will lead you to a better future,
Be open-minded, can't run away from trials,
Accept the challenge of life.

Be thankful for every blessing we received,
Everything will be done, just believe,
Be thankful in every situation,
That is the meaning of life.

HOMESICK

They are the precious gift
   I ever had,
More valuable than a gold
    On the other's hand.
They chill me up
    when I am down,
They treated me like a queen
     with an invisible crown.

They wore the sweetest smile
   I've ever seen,
Their eyes that shine,
    Oh, I can imagine.
How I wish I can watch
    how you grow,
How I wish
   I can come back tomorrow.

As I watched you growing
   day by day,
The empty space in my heart
   turning into gray.
My only prayer
   every moment,
I can overcome this homesick
   and win the tournament.

IN DANGER WORLD

Who want to reside in a world
  made of steel?
Wherein criminals and dictators,
  don't have a right to kill.
No more arguments and fighting,
No more hearts are bleeding.

The world is in danger,
The heart of humans is full of anger.
They are fighting for victory,
Others are just making history.

Where in, in a world made of steel,
All the pain, we can no longer feel.
People become immortal,
It's gone all the good moral.

No more caring, respect and love,
Even the blue skies from above.
Everything we see is metal,
Coz this world is no longer normal.

If our world made of steel,
No more virus, no one become ill.
No more stomach can feel the hunger,
And everyone will look, stranger.

So, if I ask you, my dear,
In which world do you prefer?
In a world that everywhere is dark,
Or this present where everything starts?

DREAMS AND REALITY

I never dream
to be out of their sight,
Nor letting them grow
without my guide,
But because of poverty
I pursue to work overseas,
To provide them the future
that I planned.

I set up my mind,
"I can do this," I said.
Yet I still cry,
And when I see a whole family,
The ground will be flooded instantly.

Heartbreaking scenes
when I step out of the door,
"Don't leave us, mama"
they roar.
I tried to endure the pain,
Even I can't.
So I shed my tears in silence.

I promised them
It won't be too long,
But why until now
still hoping for some changes.
"When this sacrifice will end?"

I swear upon my body,
I will bring my dreams into reality.

MY HOME, MY PARADISE

I never wished
But I dreamed,
I never ask for free
Indeed, I saved.
I never begged
Instead,
I work hard to earn.
Though I ask for help to build.

Each corner is made of hope,
Caring is mixed on the wall,
Dreams are sketched on the roof.
It is not big, not even small.
Not elegant
but it's pretty in my eye.
It is not worth a million,
But can shield
my family from the storm.
This structure is made of love.

It is surrounded by flowers
planted by my lovely mother.
Though it is not yet painted
I am already amazed.
A safe place for my kids to stay
A safe place for me to rest
when I get tired.
A safe place I called "Home",
A place that made of love.

WHO AM I?

I am a woman.
A strong woman.
A woman who has faith.
A woman who doesn't know the word hate.

A woman who accept challenges,
A woman who adopts changes.
A woman who believes in herself,
A woman who doesn't beg for help.

I failed but never give up,
I fall on the ground yet I stand up.
I got hurt and I cry,
But I learned how to fight.

So strong woman right?
But in reality, this wasn't me.
I am just the opposite version of her.
I am weak.
You may see me laughing,
But deep inside I'm crying.
I don't have enough strength to face the world.
I don't have meaning in every word.
I am just a woman
I am also human
A soft-hearted woman.

AISLES OF BROKEN VOW

You invited me
to a special place.
Colorful flowers around,
lights reflect on the ground.
Wearing an elegant dress
I walked fearlessly.

Your eyes shine like a diamond.
You look nice and adorable.
You can't express your feeling,
Yet you stay calm in midst of gathering.

While slowly walking
I kept on thinking,
The memories we had,
And moments that we shared.
The seaside where we usually seat,
And the cottage we used to sleep in.

Once we make a vow
that our love will remain,
no one can come between us.
You filled my heart with gladness
when you say I LOVE YOU
Yet in return, I give you sorrow.

I am about to reach you,
But then you stand
and went to held her hand.
I moved aside,
To give way to the bride.
She's so beautiful in white,
Only I realize,
you are no longer mine.
Into the aisles of a broken vow,
I walk without you.

PRISONER

On a dark and silent night,
I stand by my window.
Staring at the moon so bright.

I went out to walk on the meadow,
Watching the firefly that flies.
Maybe it can help me to forget my sorrow.

I closed my eyes,
Remembering those memories.
All turns gray, covered with lies.

You make my heart freeze,
You let me drown in loneliness.
Give me a reason why you do all this.

Please give back my happiness
I don't deserve to stay in darkness.

WORDS IN MY DREAM

You addressed me as a MAID,
Is it because I am cleaning your dirt?
I am paying you, that's what you said.

You let me wear a long and old skirt,
My tops are faded with long sleeves.
For you think, I am a flirt.

My hair is like falling dry leaves,
The palm of hands is as rough as sandpaper.
A living skeleton, come and count my ribs.

Life is burning hell in your hand master,
You never respect my dignity.
In this foreign land, I became a stranger.

Where is the Equality?
Our agreement was clear as water, right?
Can't your bright eyes read it carefully?

When can I have the strength to fight?
These words came only in my dreams last night.

UNEXPECTED FLAME

I was wrapped with love.
"Handle it with care, "your mother said.
As she held me to your hand,
Sun rays were visible in your eyes.
"You will decorate my life" you replied.
Your heart danced gracefully,
You're counting your step while carrying me.

You took me to a dark paradise,
The wind whispered you to unwrap me.
My pleasant scents surround,
I stared at the moon.
Inhale and exhale-you did.
I know, You're enjoying the fragrance.
You touch me slowly.
In a blink of an eye,
You light up me with flame.
I am burning,
Melting indeed.
I cried for help,
My warm tears are dropping.
Yet still
You did nothing...
You're enjoying the scene.

Did I satisfy you?
After witnessing the beauty within me,
You walk away.
You left me struggling with the fire.
But I am still lucky.,
The wind came and kiss me gently.
The fire went off,
But be careful...
Don't dare to touch me,
I am still hot,
I can burn you too.

#personification

NATURE LOVER

She admires every creature,
Exploring around completes her day.
Her eyes always look for an adventure.

A butterfly that kissing the flowers on her way,
Little birds flying while singing a lullaby.
Those scenes take her breath away.

She used to sit on the meadow while talking to the sky,
Waving to the wind, expressing her feeling.
She's whispering, I also want to fly up high.

At night when she sleeping, she's also dreaming,
High mountains and tall falls around her.
Her mind is always full of wonder.

She has a lot of memories to remember,
This lady is really a nature lover.

IF ONLY I CAN

I am looking at you from far away,
Watching your slowly falling tears.
I was standing alone, night and day.

I can see your endless nightmares,
Nor how your body was slowly giving up.
If only I can take some of your fears.

If only I could take the time to stop,
I'll come to you and hug you so tight.
But it can't, millions of miles are our gap.

I don't want to be out of your sight,
No matter how dark clouds surround me.
I will be there to be with you at night.

If only I can cross the deep blue sea,
Or even can fly like a bird in the sky.
I will come instantly to make you happy.

My love for you wasn't a lie,
If only I can, I won't say goodbye.

STARES

'Twas a devastating day
When you came and cross my way

You stared with your tantalizing eyes
But I ignore coz I thought it's full of lies

I let go of your sweet words
They might be sharp as swords

You ask for the answer to your love
But I choose to soar the sky above

I left you alone
Like a lifeless stone

You kneel in front of me
You cried and I feel guilty

I want to apologize and say sorry
Maybe I can ease a bit of your weary

I've been searching for you so long at the same place
But one day I caught you, staring at someone's face

I SURVIVED ALONE

With a grateful heart,
I tried.
I tried to keep my family unite.
But the gift of life
refused to bless me.
That moment I felt so down,
Like a queen who lost her crown.
But in the blink of an eye,
my life has changed.
Now,
I am standing like a tree.
Alone,
But strong.

Once I dreamed of a man
who can lay me on a bed of roses,
But I found a dictator
whose words are killing me softly.
I loved him more than myself.
But he tortured me.
He broke my heart into pieces.
He slapped me with his words
that full of venom,
But I survived.
I am now free as a bird.
Indeed,
I'm flying without wings.

Thou I never dream about my sweet little angels,
God send them as my special blessings.

They are the wind beneath my wings.
When my pain is in vain,
They cheer me up.
They've lightened up my life.
Their smile is glowing in the dark,
I'm just sad coz we are far apart.
I love them, fair and square.
No younger, no elder.
Thou I'm raising them alone
I know I can do it,
Coz inside of me is a heart of a lion.

My dreams are unreachable,
My wishes are impossible.
I failed hundred times,
And got hurt by sharp tongues.
I laugh so loud when I'm happy,
and I cry in silence when I'm in pain.
Those are the happenings that mold me how to be
strong.
Now I am shining like a diamond.
And I am thankful, I learned how
To survive alone.

THEY NEVER QUIT

You compared me to a turtle,

You said I am a slow mover.

But do you know how they walk?

They walk full of faith,

Their shield is courage.

They stop to rest.

A turtle

never

quit.

#nonet

YES, YOU ARE

The wind blew so cold
It touches my lonely heart
And so does your love

Singing birds that fly
Up above the clear blue sky
Brings you closed to me

In a blink of an eye
You took me out from the darkness
You're the one I wished

Your true and pure love
Makes me feel great every day
You light up my life

#multiplehaiku

SACRIFICE

I never take a long time to decide,
So right away I ask "how much should I provide?
My papers processed so fast,
I am so excited, I am flying, at last.

But why when the day comes that I must leave,
My heart feels so sad, can't believe it,
Is it real, or Am I dreaming,
My mind kept on questioning.

Is this what they called a SACRIFICE?
Should I leave to reach my dreams in life?
Do I have any choice rather than this?
Is there any way at least?

WAITING FOR THE SPRING

On a green meadow
I was standing firmly.
Enjoying the gift of love,
Embracing certain changes.
Happily dancing to the music of life.

Suddenly,
The wind blew so strong.
My colorful jewelry fell.
Teardrops fall on the ground.
What should I do?
My heart was competing with my head.
Should I follow the whisper of the wind,
Or the thunder that roaring from the sky?

I found myself amid sorrow,
Standing but lack of strength.
Weeping under the dark clouds.
As I look up to see the light,
The sun smiled at me.
It gave me hope.
I know, I can survive.
I will recover.
On the spring
I will bloom again.

#personification

GREATEST GIFTS

I suffered when you stayed in my stomach,
I carried you for a couple of months.
I cried when you can't wait to come out,
I sacrifice yet I survived, I delivered safely.

I always tickle your tiny toes,
Your cute and chubby cheeks I loved to pinch.
You let me learn to love and care,
You relieve my stress by smiling so sweet.

When you simply sad or suddenly scared,
You crawl so fast to come and cuddle me.
You hide when you saw the sun shining,
You giggle when green leaves waves at you.

I promise to protect and pray for you,
Time can't stop me to show how I Love You.
You can comfort me anytime and anywhere,
You are my greatest gift from God.

ODE TO WHITE SANDY BEACH

Oh white sandy beach
You have a breathtaking view,
You make my eyes stuck on you.

Oh white sandy beach
The quiet sounds of your sea,
Took away all my sorrows and weariness.

Oh white sandy beach
As I walk with you without my shoes,
You run after me and tickle my toes.

Oh white sandy beach
I want to caress your body,
But I cant you're running away from me.

Oh white sandy beach
I want to stay with you until noon,
But I can't coz we are leaving soon.

ODE TO MYSELF

I saw the delights in your alluring eyes,
You are like an angel in disguise.
I love those point of view that you wears,
Although sometimes your peer disappears.
Your smile blazed like the sun,
You talk humbly to everyone.
Even you're exhausted you're still working,
Unending support you are giving.
I know occasionally you're failing,
Yet it doesn't matter, you're still fighting.
Keep shining even in darkness,
I am wishing you all the best.

ODE TO MY MOTHER

Mother dear I love you so,
Thank you for being my shadow.
I am so blessed to be your child,
You teach me how to act with humankind.
Your sweet smile, I always remember,
Yet soft-hearted but never surrender.
Your metallic bones lifted me up
You carried me until now without a stop.
Time, days, and years may pass,
But your love will never last.
Thank you mother for every sweat,
You worked for us from sunrise till sunset.
Now that you're age is catching up,
Let us be the one to lift you up.
I want to say I am so sorry,
For being stubborn, sometimes naughty,
I promised I will behave like how you want me to be.
Mother dear thank you for my life,
Thank you for all the sacrifice.

HUGS, KISSES, AND TEARS

It's time again to leave,
Not because I want
but because I need to.
My heart is writhing in pain,
I don't want to be separated from you.
I could do nothing but cry,
coz I know,
my return is uncertain.

Goodbye, my dear,
Feel the warmth of my embrace,
Though It brings emotional joy.

Even if the sea and mountains are between us,
Don't worry I won't change,
I will come back and never leave again.

Oh, how sweet is your kiss.
Day and night I will be longing for you.
Just think I love you so much.
Even if you are far away,
I will not look at others.
I will always remember
your promises.
That you and me,
forever.

JUST ENJOY THE JOURNEY

Life is a short journey to enjoy,
Don't let anyone destroy.
Walk slowly, don't run.
Be yourself, have some fun.

Sometimes it's bumpy, a lot of challenges.
Sometimes flooded, strength is less.
No matter what, keep going silently.
Just believe, it will flow gently.

If you are tired, stop and rest.
Do not rush and end up with a mess.
Follow the main road, not the shortcut,
Otherwise, you will lose and get stuck.

Success may seem so far
But be patient 'till you reach the star.
You may struggle on your way a lot,
Yet at the end, the rainbow is on the spot.

DON'T STOP ON BLOOMING

I am just like a tiny flower,
Living in a world of wonder.
I was surrounded by beauties,
And I don't know who's my enemies.
I was enjoying relaxing and rejoicing,
Not knowing when is my ending.
Sometimes I am scared of my own shadow,
So I just go on with the flow.
But when the sun smiles at me,
It takes away all my worry.
This world may full of mysteries,
Yet we must appreciate every piece.
Thou I am just a tiny flower,
I won't stop on blooming, rain, or shine it doesn't matter.

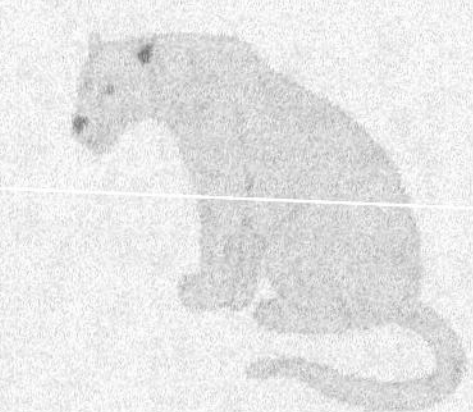

QADAMA IN KSA

You were wrapped clothed.
Can't even see the circle of your eyes. Every single
move, deliberately watched,
Wiping away even invisible dust.

Under the flammable sun,
you are exposed.
Your fatigue and sorrow are unparalleled.
There is no space for your grievances, They never think
that you are also a creature.

In the dark and small room,
you've been isolated.
Do they have no heart
Or are they deliberately numb.

With food and rest
you are always deficient,
Your only wealth is your own bones and skin.

Why my fate is so bitter?
Why is the world so cruel to me? Questions you keep
repeating, Especially when problems appearing.

You've been Insulted and enslaved.
With a little patience, suffering will end.

ABANDONED DREAM

A quiet atmosphere
A deafening silence
How pleasant to breathe
And sniffed the fragrant breeze.

I waited for you
My own body, I caressed.
My mind full of doubt,
are you coming back.

Savoring my own tears,
my heart is in pain
but avoids feeling resentment.

By the time I open my eyes,
I wish it was morning.
I don't want to feel the bitterness anymore.

The pain,
I felt while waiting.
Here in our dream castle,
you abandoned me.

SUNSET

An amazing view.
A perfect creation of our Creator,
created with a figure that glazed.

Since I was a child
I've been your fans
Standing,
watching while your stunts.
I always wondered
why at night you're gone,
Only realized that
another day is done.

I won't last the day
Without staring at you,
Hoping that tomorrow again
I'll see you through,
Oh sun that setting down
let me feel,
That your presence,
in my heart is real.

Oh sun that setting down
how I wish you can hear,
All the sorrows and pain
I whispered with a tear.
Please take some
and flamed it with your gas,
Burn it nicely.
Turn them into dust.

NEVER STOP

Life is an unstoppable journey.

Trials are always on our way

We may get tired or failed

Sometimes humiliated

But no matter what,

Do not give up

Reach that dream.

Never

stop.

#nonet

ABOUT THE AUTHOR

"The wondrous sky witnessed every failure and success of every creature".

"Never abuse the kindness of a woman. Once she stepped out of the door, she may never come back."-

Kristine Andaya Ventura is from Jones, Isabela, Philippines. She's a mother of two kids and a Quite Warrior. She is a Domestic Helper in Malaysia From 2016 to the present, staying with the same employer. She is also a Team Leader of a non-profit organization named Uplifters and from there, she cultivated he passion for writing. With the help of her fellow migrant writers and a group of empowered ladies named "CINDERELLA'S ANGELS", she learned different poetic devices and forms which she applied in this book.

Despite being a single parent, Kristine never gave up her dreams. Her kids are her source of strength. She played the role of a mother and a father at the same time without any doubt. Trials and burdens are always waving on her but she remains still.

Her passion for writing helped her to gain the confidence that she used to fight in every battle of life. By dropping all her emotions that she can't voice out, she found her inner peace. She is also sharing some of her poems in different groups of poetry. Reading and sketching sometimes fade her longing for her loved ones left behind.

www.ingramcontent.com/pod-product-compliance
Lightning Source LLC
LaVergne TN
LVHW012050200726

843506LV00023BA/2847